This book
was presented

to

_____

by

_____

on

_____

My Favorite
Bible Songs

Art Direction by Danny Brooks Dalby
Designed by Tatia M. Lockridge
Sheet music arranged by Justin Peters

Published in 2005 by Spirit Press, an imprint of Dalmatian Press LLC

Copyright © 2005, Dalmatian Press, LLC. All rights reserved.

ISBN: 1-40371-603-X (B)
1-40371-757-5 (S)
14399

Printed in the U.S.A.

05 06 07 08 LBM 10 9 8 7 6 5 4 3 2 1

My Favorite
Bible Songs

Make a joyful noise

unto the LORD,

all ye lands.

Serve the LORD with

gladness; come

before His presence

with singing.

—Psalm 100:1-2

My Favorite BIBLE SONGS

Illustrated by Tom Newsom

SPIRIT PRESS

Jesus Loves Me

Words: Anna B. Warner

Music: William B. Bradbury

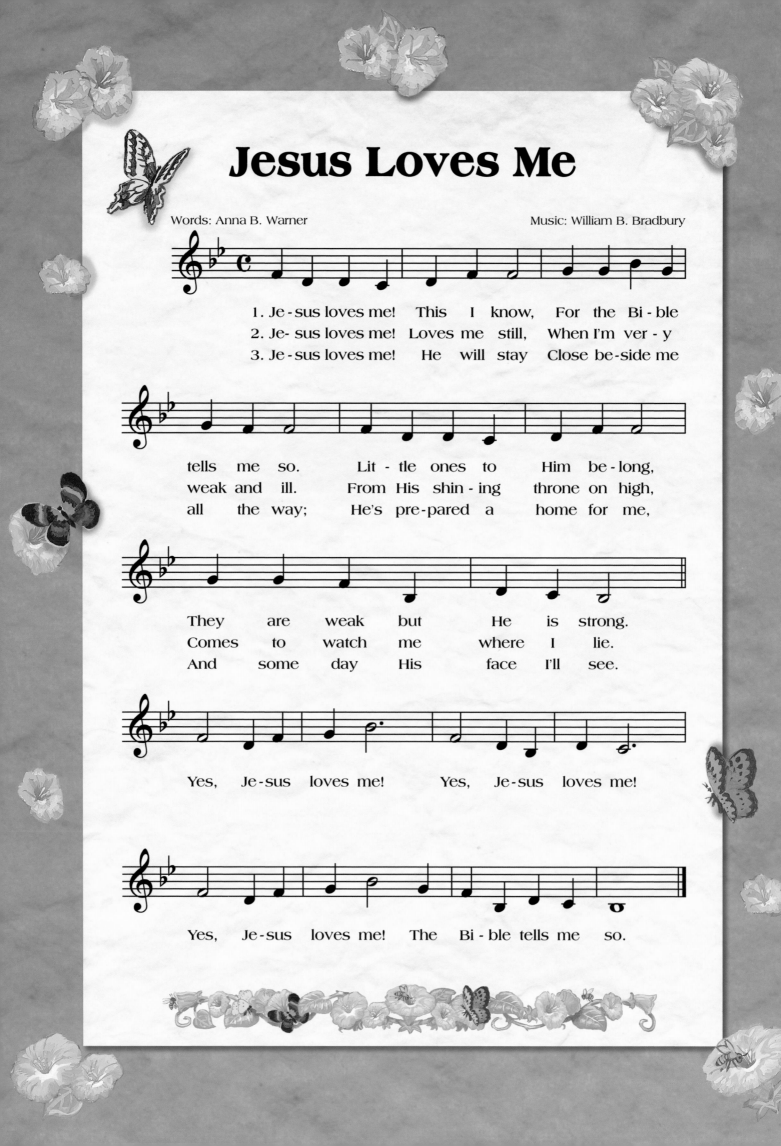

This Little Light of Mine

Words and Music: Harry Dixon Loes

1. This lit- tle light of mine,   I'm gon-na let it shine.
2. Hide it   un-der a bush-el? NO! I'm gon-na let it shine.
3. Don't let   Sat - an blow it out! I'm gon-na let it shine.

This   lit - tle   light   of mine,   I'm gon-na let it   shine.
Hide   it   un-der a   bush-el? NO! I'm gon-na let it   shine.
Don't let   Sat - an blow it out! I'm gon-na let it   shine.

This   lit - tle light   of mine,   I'm gon-na let it shine, let it
Hide   it   un-der a bush-el? NO! I'm gon-na let it shine, let it
Don't let   Sat - an blow it out! I'm gon-na let it shine, let it

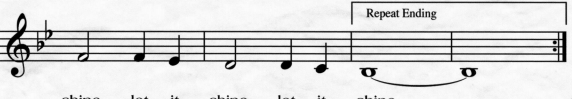

Repeat Ending

shine,   let   it   shine,   let   it   shine._____

Last time

shine._____ Let it   shine, let it   shine, let it   shine._____

He shall come down

like rain upon

the mown grass:

as showers that

water the earth.

. . .

Let the whole earth

be filled

with His glory.

—Psalm 72:6,19

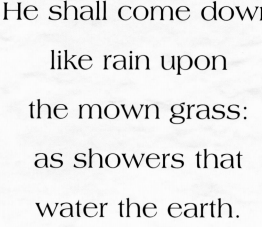
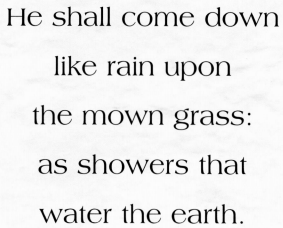
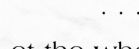

He's Got the Whole World In His Hands

Traditional

1. He's got the whole world _____ in His hands! He's got the

whole world _____ in His hands! He's got the whole world _____

in His hands! He's got the whole world in His hands! 2. He's got

you and me, broth-er, in His hands! He's got you and me sis-ter,
lit - tle bit-ty ba-by in His hands! He's got the lit - tle bit-ty ba-by

in His hands! He's got you and me, broth-er, in His hands! He's got the
in His hands! He's got the lit - tle bit-ty ba - by in His hands! He's got the

Repeat ending | Last time

whole world in His hands! 3. He's got the hands!

Count Your Blessings

Words: Johnson Oatman, Jr.

Music: Edwin O. Excell

Count your bless-ings, name them one by one;

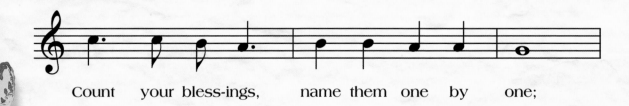

Count your bless-ings, see what God has done;

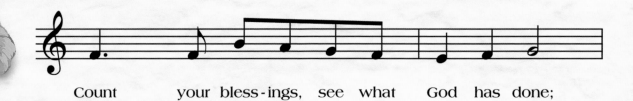

Count your bless-ings, name them one by one;

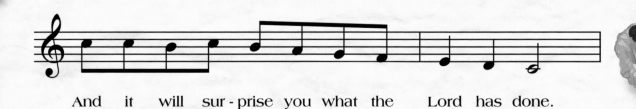

And it will sur-prise you what the Lord has done.

And it will sur-prise you what the Lord has done.

Zacchaeus Was a Wee Little Man

Traditional

1. Za - cchae-us was a wee lit-tle man, A wee lit-tle man was

he.   He   climbed up in the syc-a-more tree, the Sav-ior for to

see.   2. And   when   the Sav-ior passed that way, He

looked up   in   the   tree,   And He said,   "Za-cchae-us, you

come down from there; For I'm go-ing to your house to - day."

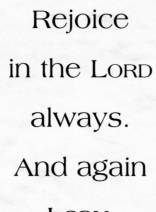

Rejoice

in the Lᴏʀᴅ

always.

And again

I say,

Rejoice!

—Philippians 4:4

Down In My Heart

Words and Music: George Cooke

1. I've got the joy, joy, joy, joy
2. I've got the peace that pass-es un - der - stand-ing
3. I've got the love of Je - sus, love of Je - sus,

down in my heart, down in my heart, down in my heart. I've got the
down in my heart, down in my heart, down in my heart. I've got the
down in my heart, down in my heart, down in my heart. I've got the

joy, joy, joy, joy down in my heart,
peace that pass - es un - der - stand-ing down in my heart,
love of Je - sus, love of Je - sus, down in my heart,

Repeat twice last time

down in my heart to stay.
down in my heart to stay.
down in my heart to stay.

Tell Me the Stories of Jesus

Words: William H. Parker

Music: Frederick A. Challinor

1. Tell me the sto-ries of Je-sus   I   love   to   hear;
2. First let me hear how the chil-dren stood 'round His   knee,
3. In - to the cit - y I'd fol-low The   chil-dren's band,

Things I would ask Him to   tell me   If He were here:
And   I shall fan - cy His bless-ing Rest-ing on   me;
Wav - ing   a   branch of the palm tree High in my hand;

Scenes   by   the   way - side,   Tales   of   the   sea,
Words   full   of   kind - ness,   Deeds   full   of   grace,
One   of   His   her - alds,   Yes,   I   would   sing

Sto - ries   of   Je - sus,   Tell   them   to   me.
All   in   the   love - light   Of   Je - sus'   face.
Loud - est ho - san - nas,   "Je - sus   is   King!"

The B-I-B-L-E

Traditional

The   B-I-B-L E!   Yes, that's the book for me!   I

stand a-lone on the word of God, the   B-I-B-L-E!   The

B-I-B-L-E!   I stand a-lone on the word of God, the

B-I-B-L-E!

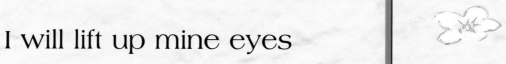

I will lift up mine eyes

unto the hills,

from whence

cometh my help.

My help cometh

from the Lord,

Which made heaven

and earth.

—*Psalm 121:1-2*

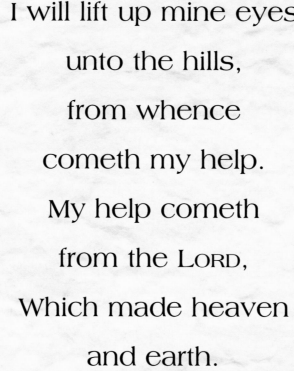

Deep and Wide

Traditional

Deep and wide, Deep and wide. There's a

Foun - tain flow - ing deep and wide!

Deep and wide, Deep and wide. There's a

Foun - tain flow - ing deep and wide!

Jesus Loves
the Little Children

Words and Music: George F. Root

1. Je - sus   loves   the lit - tle   chil - dren,
2. Je - sus   lives   for all   the   chil - dren,

All   the   chil - dren of   the   world;   Red   and
All   the   chil - dren of   the   world;   Red   and

yel-low, black and white, They are pre-cious in his sight; Je - sus
yel-low, black and white, They are pre-cious in his sight; Je - sus

loves   the lit - tle chil - dren of   the   world.
lives   for all   the chil - dren of   the   world.

Praise ye the Lord.

Praise the Lord,

O my soul.

While I live will I

praise the Lord.

—*Psalm 146:1-2*